COPPER SUN

COPPER SUN

DOVER THRIFT EDITIONS

Countee Cullen

With Decorations by
Charles Cullen

DOVER PUBLICATIONS
GARDEN CITY, NEW YORK

DOVER THRIFT EDITIONS

GENERAL EDITOR: SUSAN L. RATTINER
EDITOR OF THIS VOLUME: MICHAEL CROLAND

This Dover edition, first published in 2023, is an unabridged republication of the work, originally published by Harper & Brothers, Publishers, New York, in 1927. A new introductory Note has been specially prepared for this edition.

Library of Congress Cataloging-in-Publication Data

Names: Cullen, Countee, 1903–1946, author. | Cullen, Charles, illustrator.
Title: Copper sun / Countee Cullen ; with decorations by Charles Cullen.
Description: Dover edition. | Garden City, New York : Dover Publications, 2023. | Series: Dover thrift editions | Summary: "Countee Cullen explores the emotional consequences of race, religion, and sexuality in Jazz Age America in his moving, eloquent, and poignant poems"—Provided by publisher.
Identifiers: LCCN 2023018227 | ISBN 9780486852027 (trade paperback) | ISBN 0486852024 (trade paperback)
Subjects: LCGFT: Poetry.
Classification: LCC PS3505.U287 C65 2023 | DDC 811/.52—dc23/eng/20230522
LC record available at https://lccn.loc.gov/2023018227

Manufactured in the United States of America
85202401   2023
www.doverpublications.com

To the Not Impossible Her

Note

COUNTEE CULLEN WAS born in 1903, likely in Louisville, Kentucky. He later moved to New York City, where he edited his high school's newspaper and literary magazine. He began writing poetry at fourteen. After winning a citywide poetry competition as a teenager, his verse was widely reprinted.

Cullen attended New York University, where he won the Witter Bynner Poetry Prize. While he was in college, his poems frequently appeared in major literary magazines. He published his debut poetry collection, *Color*, in 1925, the same year that he graduated with a bachelor's degree. He received a master's degree in English from Harvard University in 1926.

Cullen's sophomore poetry book, *Copper Sun* (1927), helped establish him as a leading figure in the Black literary and art movement known as the Harlem Renaissance. *The New York Times* said that *Copper Sun* "reveals a profounder depth than *Color*." *Copper Sun* opens with one of Cullen's best-known poems, "From the Dark Tower," which was the namesake of his "Dark Tower" column in *Opportunity* magazine.

Race, faith, and especially love are common subjects in *Copper Sun*. Many poems address "romantic love, in all its transcendence and tortuous intensity, whether fulfilled or unrequited," noted Charles Molesworth in his biography of Cullen, *And Bid Him Sing*. Molesworth added, "Many of the poems in *Copper Sun* contribute to Cullen's spiritual and emotional autobiography, and they are less flavored with the schoolbook techniques and rhymes of [Cullen's] earlier poetry, though they retain their commitment to high lyricism and a vocabulary of transcendence."

Cullen's other works include the poetry books *The Ballad of the Brown Girl* (1927) and *The Black Christ and Other Poems* (1929) as well as the novel *One Way to Heaven* (1932). He compiled *Caroling Dusk* (1927), a seminal anthology of Harlem Renaissance poetry. Cullen was also a playwright and children's book author, and he taught French at a junior high school.

Cullen passed away in 1946. *On These I Stand: An Anthology of the Best Poems of Countee Cullen* was published posthumously the next year.

Contents

Acknowledgments

To

Harper's Magazine
Poetry: A Magazine Of Verse
Opportunity: Journal Of Negro Life
Palms
The Crisis
Fire
Folio
Yule Tide Anthology
The Measure
Vanity Fair
Books of *The New York Herald-Tribune*
Foot Prints
The Conning Tower of the *New York World*
The Nation
The Bookman
The Carolina Magazine

acknowledgment is hereby made for permission to reprint certain poems that first appeared in these periodicals.

COPPER SUN

Color

From the Dark Tower

(*To Charles S. Johnson*)

We shall not always plant while others reap
The golden increment of bursting fruit,
Not always countenance, abject and mute,
That lesser men should hold their brothers cheap;
Not everlastingly while others sleep
Shall we beguile their limbs with mellow flute,
Not always bend to some more subtle brute;
We were not made eternally to weep.

The night whose sable breast relieves the stark,
White stars is no less lovely being dark,
And there are buds that cannot bloom at all
In light, but crumple, piteous, and fall;
So in the dark we hide the heart that bleeds,
And wait, and tend our agonizing seeds.

Threnody for a Brown Girl

Weep not, you who love her;
What rebellious flow
Grief undams shall recover
Whom the gods bid go?
Sorrow rising like a wall,
Bitter, blasphemous,
What avails it to recall
Beauty back to us?

Think not this grave shall keep her,
This marriage-bed confine;
Death may dig it deep and deeper;
She shall climb it like a vine.
Body that was quick and sentient,
Dear as thought or speech,
Death could not with one trenchant
Blow snatch out of reach.

She is nearer than the word
Wasted on her now,
Nearer than the swaying bird
On its rhythmic bough.
Only were our faith as much
As a mustard seed,
Aching, hungry hands might touch
Her as they touch a reed.

Life who was not loth to trade her
Unto death, has done
Better than he planned, has made her
Wise as Solomon.
Now she knows the Why and Wherefore,
Troublous Whence and Whither,
Why men strive and sweat, and care for
Bays that droop and wither.

All the stars she knows by name,
End and origin thereof,
Knows if love be kin to shame,
If shame be less than love.
What was crooked now is straight,
What was rough is plain;
Grief and sorrow have no weight
Now to cause her pain.

Plain to her why fevered blisters
Made her dark hands run,
While her favored, fairer sisters
Neither wrought nor spun;
Clear to her the hidden reason
Men daily fret and toil,
Staving death off for a season
Till soil return to soil.

One to her are flame and frost;
Silence is her singing lark;
We alone are children, lost,
Crying in the dark.
Varied feature now, and form,
Change has bred upon her;
Crush no bug nor nauseous worm
Lest you tread upon her.

Pluck no flower lest she scream;
Bruise no slender reed,
Lest it prove more than it seem,
Lest she groan and bleed.
More than ever trust your brother,
Read him golden, pure;
It may be she finds no other
House so safe and sure.

Set no poet carving
Rhymes to make her laugh;
Only live hearts starving
Need an epitaph.
Lay upon her no white stone
From a foreign quarry;
Earth and sky be these alone
Her obituary.

Swift as startled fawn or swallow,
Silence all her sound,
She has fled; we cannot follow
Further than this mound.
We who take the beaten track
Trying to appease
Hearts near breaking with their lack,
We need elegies.

Confession

If for a day joy masters me,
Think not my wounds are healed;
Far deeper than the scars you see,
I keep the roots concealed.

They shall bear blossoms with the fall;
I have their word for this,
Who tend my roots with rains of gall,
And suns of prejudice.

Uncle Jim

"White folks is white," says uncle Jim;
"A platitude," I sneer;
And then I tell him so is milk,
And the froth upon his beer.

His heart walled up with bitterness,
He smokes his pungent pipe,
And nods at me as if to say,
"Young fool, you'll soon be ripe!"

I have a friend who eats his heart
Away with grief of mine,
Who drinks my joy as tipplers drain
Deep goblets filled with wine.

I wonder why here at his side,
Face-in-the-grass with him,
My mind should stray the Grecian urn
To muse on uncle Jim.

Colored Blues Singer

Some weep to find the Golden Pear
Feeds maggots at the core,
And some grow cold as ice, and bear
Them prouder than before.

But you go singing like the sea
Whose lover turns to land;
You make your grief a melody
And take it by the hand.

Such songs the mellow-bosomed maids
Of Africa intone
For lovers dead in hidden glades,
Slow rotting flesh and bone.

Such keenings tremble from the kraal,
Where sullen-browed abides
The second wife whose dark tears fail
To draw him to her sides.

Somewhere Jeritza breaks her heart
On symbols Verdi wrote;
You tear the strings of your soul apart,
Blood dripping note by note.

Colors

(*To Leland*)

(Red)

She went to buy a brand new hat,
And she was ugly, black, and fat:
"This red becomes you well," they said,
And perched it high upon her head.
And then they laughed behind her back
To see it glow against the black.
She paid for it with regal mien,
And walked out proud as any queen.

(Black)

1

The play is done, the crowds depart; and see
That twisted tortured thing hung from a tree,
Swart victim of a newer Calvary.

2

Yea, he who helped Christ up Golgotha's track,
That Simon who did *not* deny, was black.

(The Unknown Color)

I've often heard my mother say,
When great winds blew across the day,
And, cuddled close and out of sight,
The young pigs squealed with sudden fright
Like something speared or javelined,
"Poor little pigs, they see the wind."

The Litany of the Dark People

Our flesh that was a battle-ground
Shows now the morning-break;
The ancient deities are downed
For Thy eternal sake.
Now that the past is left behind,
Fling wide Thy garment's hem
To keep us one with Thee in mind,
Thou Christ of Bethlehem.

The thorny wreath may ridge our brow,
The spear may mar our side,
And on white wood from a scented bough
We may be crucified;
Yet no assault the old gods make
Upon our agony
Shall swerve our footsteps from the wake
Of Thine toward Calvary.

And if we hunger now and thirst,
Grant our withholders may,
When heaven's constellations burst
Upon Thy crowning day,
Be fed by us, and given to see
Thy mercy in our eyes,
When Bethlehem and Calvary
Are merged in Paradise.

The Deep in Love

Pity the Deep in Love

(To Fiona)

Pity the deep in love;
They move as men asleep,
Traveling a narrow way
Precipitous and steep.
Tremulous is the lover's breath
With little moans and sighs;
Heavy are the brimming lids
Upon a lover's eyes.

One Day We Played a Game

(*Yolande: Her Poem*)

One day we lay beneath an apple tree,
Tumultuous with fruit, live with the bee,
And there we played a gay, fantastic game
Of our own making, called Name me a Name.
The grave was liberal, letting us endow
Ourselves with names of lovers who by now
Are dust, but rarer dust for loving high
Than they shall be who let the red flame die. . . .
Crouched sphinx-wise in the grass, you hugged your knees,
And called me "Abelard"; I, "Heloise,"
Rejoined, and added thereto, "Melisande";
Then "Pelleas," I heard, and felt a hand
Slide into mine; joy would not let us speak
Awhile, but only sit there cheek to cheek,
Hand clasping hand. . . . till passion made us bold;
"Tristan," you purred to me. . . . I laughed, "Isolde."
"King Ninus, I," I cried; snared in a kiss
You named yourself my dark Semiramis.
"Queen Guinevere," I sang; you, "Lancelot."
My heart grew big with pride to think you'd not
Cried "Arthur," whom his lovely queen forgot
In loving him whose name you called me by. . . .
We two grew mad with loving then, and I
With whirlpool rapture strained you to my breast;
"First love! First love!" I urged, and "Adam!" blessed
My urgency. My lips grew soft with "Eve,"
And round with ardor purposing to leave
Upon your mouth a lasting seal of bliss. . . .
But midway of our kissing came a hiss
Above us in the apple tree; a sweet
Red apple rolled between us at our feet,
And looking up we saw with glide and dip,
Cold supple coils among the branches slip.
"Eve! Eve!" I cried, "Beware!" Too late. You bit
Half of the fruit away. . . . The rest of it
I took, assuring you with misty eyes,
"Fare each as each, we lose no Paradise."

Timid Lover

I who employ a poet's tongue,
Would tell you how
You are a golden damson hung
Upon a silver bough.

I who adore exotic things
Would shape a sound
To be your name, a word that sings
Until the head goes round.

I who am proud with other folk
Would grow complete
In pride on bitter words you spoke,
And kiss your petalled feet.

But never past the frail intent
My will may flow,
Though gentle looks of yours are bent
Upon me where I go.

So must I, starved for love's delight,
Affect the mute,
When love's divinest acolyte
Extends me holy fruit.

Nocturne

Tell me all things false are true,
Bitter sweet, that fools are wise;
I will not doubt nor question you;
I am in a mood for lies.

Tell me all things ill turn good;
Thew and sinew will be stronger
Thriving on the deadly food
Life proffers for their hunger.

Paint love lovely, if you will;
Be crafty, sly, deceptive;
Here is fertile land to till,
Sun-seeking, rain-receptive.

Hold my hand and lie to me;
I will not ask you How nor Why;
I see death drawing nigh to me
Out of the corner of my eye.

Words to My Love

What if you come
Again and swell
The throat of some
Mute bird;
How shall I tell?
How shall I know
That it is so,
Having heard?

Love, let no trick
Of what's to come
Deceive; the quick
So soon grow dumb;
With wine and bread
Our feast is spread;
Let's leave no crumb.

En Passant

If I was born a liar, lass,
And you were born a jade,
It's just the way things come to pass,
And men and mice are made.

I tell you love is like the dew
That trembles on the grass;
You'd not believe me, speaking true,
That love is wormwood, lass.

You swear no other lips but mine
Have clung like this to yours,
But lass, I know how such strong wine
Draws bees and flies by scores.

I now voluptuously bask
Where Jack tomorrow will,
And while we kiss, I long to ask,
"What girl goes up that hill?"

You love me for the liar I am;
I love the minx you are;
'Tis heaven we must bless or damn
That shaped us on a par.

Variations on a Theme

(*The Loss of Love*)

1

This house where Love a little while abode,
Impoverished completely of him now,
Of every vestige bare, drained like a bough
Wherefrom the all-sustaining sap has flowed
Away, yet bears upon its front bestowed
A cabalistic legend telling how
Love for a meagre space deigned to allow
It summer scent before the winter snowed.
Here rots to ruin a splendor proudly calm,
A skeleton whereof the clean bones wear
Their indigence relieved of any qualm
For purple robes that once were folded there.
The mouldy Coliseum draws upon
Our wonder yet . . . no less Love's Parthenon.

2

All through an empty place I go,
And find her not in any room;
The candles and the lamps I light
Go down before a wind of gloom.

Thick-spraddled lies the dust about,
A fit, sad place to write her name
Or draw her face the way she looked
That legendary night she came.

The old house crumbles bit by bit;
Each day I hear the ominous thud
That says another rent is there
For winds to pierce and storms to flood,

My orchards groan and sag with fruit;
Where, Indian-wise, the bees go round;
I let it rot upon the bough;
I eat what falls upon the ground.

The heavy cows go laboring
In agony with clotted teats;
My hands are slack; my blood is cold;
I marvel that my heart still beats.

I have no will to weep or sing,
No least desire to pray or curse;
The loss of love is a terrible thing;
They lie who say that death is worse.

A Song of Sour Grapes

I wish your body were in the grave,
Deep down as a grave may be,
Or rotting under the deepest wave
That ever ploughed the sea.

I wish I never had seen your face,
Or the sinuous curve of your mouth,
Dear as a straw to a man who drowns
Or rain to a land in drouth.

I would that your mother had never borne,
Your father's seed to fruit,
That meadow rats had gnawed his corn
Before it gathered root.

In Memoriam

You were the path I had to take
  To find that all
That lay behind its loops and bends
  Was a bare blank wall.

You were the way my curious hands
  Were doomed to learn
That fire, lovely to the sight,
  To the touch will burn.

That yours was no slight rôle, my dear,
  Be well content;
Not everyone is blessed to be
  Wisdom's instrument.

Lament

Now let all lovely things embark
Upon the sea of mist
With her whose luscious mouth the dark,
Grim troubadour has kissed.

The silver clock that ticked away
Her days, and never knew
Its beats were sword thrusts to the clay
That too much beauty slew.

The pillow favored with her tears
And hallowed by her head;
I shall not even keep my fears,
Now their concern is dead.

But where shall I bury sun and rain,
How mortalise the stars,
How still the half-heard cries of pain
That seared her soul with scars?

In what sea depths shall all the seeds
Of every flower die?
Where shall I scatter the broken reeds,
And how erase the sky?

And where shall I find a hole so deep
No troubled ghost may rise?
There will I put my heart to sleep
Wanting her face and eyes.

If Love Be Staunch

If love be staunch, call mountains brittle;
Love is a thing will live
So long, my dear,—oh, just the little
While water stays in a sieve.

Yea, love is deathless as the day
Whose death the stars reveal;
And love is loyal all the way,
If treachery be leal.

Beyond the shadow of a doubt,
No thing is sweet as love,
But, oh, the bitterness spewed out
Of the heart at the end thereof!

Beyond all cavil or complaint,
Love's ways are double-dyed;
Beneath the surplice of a saint
The cloven hooves are spied.

Whom yesterday love rhymed his sun
Today he names a star;
When the course of another day is run,
What will he say you are?

The Spark

Stamp hard, be sure
We leave no spark
That may allure
This placid dark.
At last we learn
That love is cruel;
Fire will not burn
Lacking fuel.

Here, take your heart,
The whole of it;
I want no part,
No smallest bit.
And this is mine?
You took scant care;
My heart could *shine;*
No glaze was there.

Young lips hold wine
The fair world over;
New heads near mine
Will dent the clover;
We need not pine
Now this is over.

Now love is dead
We might be friends;
'Tis best instead
To say all ends,
And when we meet
Pass quickly by;
Oh, speed your feet,
And so will I.

I know a man
Thought a spark was dead
That flamed and ran
A brighter red,
And burned the roof
Above his head.

Song of the Rejected Lover

With silver bell scarce sounding at the pace,
Slow riding down from courtly Camelot,
Roused from the splendor of her escort's grace,
Queen Guinevere turns cold to Lancelot.

For love of me Elaine has kissed Death's face,
For love of me is grief in Astolat,
While for the warm delight of my embrace
Queen Guinevere turns cold to Lancelot.

Thou slender cruelty and slim distress,
Let each to each forgetful and forgot
Abide; for me, a dream-dark loveliness,
Queen Guinevere turns cold to Lancelot.

To One Who Was Cruel

The wound you gave
Will not abide,
Nor what you crave
Be gratified.

Time with deft finger
Probing far,
Will let linger
No sign or scar.

Only a line like snow,
So faint, so thin,
Folks will not know
A wound has been.

Sonnet to a Scornful Lady

(To Ruth Marie)

Like some grim gladiator who has fought
Men loving life as lustily as he,
And with red wounds and blood has dearly bought
A forced reprieve from those who came to see
Him die; a suppliant on gory knees
Like him, lean with my passion's hunger, I
Lay bare the bruises of my heart, with these
Imploring, "Love me, lady, or I die."

But unlike him I hear no populace
Enamoured of a brave bout, crying, "Grace!"
Scorn rules your eyes as silence does your mouth;
No golden sceptre raises me from where
I kneel unfavored finding you still fair
Though both your regal thumbs are pointed south.

The Love Tree

Come, let us plant our love as farmers plant
A seed, and you shall water it with tears,
And I shall weed it with my hands until
They bleed. Perchance this buried love of ours
Will fall on goodly ground and bear a tree
With fruit and flowers; pale lovers chancing here
May pluck and eat, and through their veins a sweet
And languid ardor play, their pulses beat
An unimagined tune, their shy lips meet
And part, and bliss repeat again. And men
Will pilgrimage from far and wide to see
This tree for which we two were crucified,
And, happy in themselves, will never know
'Twas break of heart that made the Love Tree grow.

At Cambridge

(With grateful appreciation to Robert S. Hillyer)

The Wind Bloweth Where It Listeth

"Live like the wind," he said, "unfettered,
  And love me while you can;
And when you will, and can be bettered,
  Go to the better man.

"For you'll grow weary, maybe, sleeping
  So long a time with me;
Like this there'll be no cause for weeping;
  The wind is always free.

"Go when you please," he would be saying,
  His mouth hard on her own;
That's why she stayed and loved the staying,
  Contented to the bone.

And now he's dust, and he but twenty,—
  Frost that was like a flame;
Her kisses on the head death bent, he
  Gave answer to his name.

And now he's dust and with dust lying
  In sullen arrogance;
Death found it hard, for all his trying,
  To shatter such a lance.

She laid him out as fine as any
  That had a priest and ring;
She never spared a silver penny
  For cost of anything.

Her grief is crowned with his child sucking
  The milk of her distress,
As if his father's hands were plucking
  Her buds of bitterness.

He may grow tall as any other,
  Blest with his father's face,
And yield her strength enough to smother
  What some will call disgrace.

He may be cursed and be concerned
  With thoughts of right and wrong,
And brand with "Shame" these two that burned
  Without the legal thong.

Her man would say they were no rabble
  To love like common clay,—
But Christian tongues are trained to babble
  In such a bitter way.

Still, she's this minted gold to pour her,
  This from her man for a mark:
It was no law that held him for her,
  And moved his feet in the dark.

Thoughts in a Zoo

They in their cruel traps, and we in ours,
Survey each other's rage, and pass the hours
Commiserating each the other's woe,
To mitigate his own pain's fiery glow.
Man could but little proffer in exchange
Save that his cages have a larger range.
That lion with his lordly, untamed heart
Has in some man his human counterpart,
Some lofty soul in dreams and visions wrapped,
But in the stifling flesh securely trapped.
Gaunt eagle whose raw pinions stain the bars
That prison you, so men cry for the stars!
Some delve down like the mole far underground,
(Their nature is to burrow, not to bound),
Some, like the snake, with changeless slothful eye,
Stir not, but sleep and smoulder where they lie.
Who is most wretched, these caged ones, or we,
Caught in a vastness beyond our sight to see?

Two Thoughts of Death

1

When I am dead, it will not be
Much matter of concern to me
Who folds my hands, or combs my hair,
Or, pitying their sightless stare,
Draws down the blinds across my eyes.
I shall not have the least surmise
Which of the many loves I had
Weeps most the passing of her lad.
Not what these give, nor what they keep,
Shall gladden or disturb my sleep,
If only one who never guessed
How every tremor in her breast
Reverberated in my own.
In that last hour come and bend down
To kiss my long-expectant mouth
Still curved, in death, to meet her mouth.

2

I am content to play the martyr,
To wear the dunce cap here at school;
For every tear I shed I'll barter
To Death; I'll be no more a fool
When that pale rider reaches down
His hand to me. He'll beat a crown
From all the aches my shoulders bore,
And I shall lord one regal hour
Illumined in all things before
His sickle spears another flower.
While still his shears snarl through my thread,
Dismembering it strand by strand,
While I hang poised between the dead
And quick, into omniscience fanned,
My mind shall glow with one rich spark
Before it ends in endless dark.

These straining eyes, clairvoyant then,
Shall probe beneath the calloused husk
That hides the better selves of men.
And as my day throbs into dusk,
This heart the world has made to bleed,
While all its red stream deathward flows,
Shall comprehend just why the seed
Must agonize to be the rose.

The Poet Puts His Heart to School

Our love has dwindled down to this:
With proper stress and emphasis
To crown a given exercise;
Those lips, that bearing, those great eyes
I once was wont to praise, I trade
Now for technique and for a grade.
That sun in which I used to bask
Now glorifies a schoolboy's task.
Priest am I now for wisdom's pay,
And half a priest's task is to slay,
Nor raise one far-remembering cry
Though with the slain the slayer die.
Aloft the sacred knife is curved:
The gods of knowledge must be served.

Love's Way

Love is not love demanding all, itself
Withholding aught; love's is the nobler way
Of courtesy, that will not feast aware
That the beloved hungers, nor drink unless
The cup be shared down to the last sweet dregs.
Renunciatory never was the thorn
To crown love with, but *prodigal* and *proud!*
Too proud to rest the debtor of the one
Dear passion most it dotes upon, always
Love rehabilitates unto the end.
So let it be with us; the perfect faith
We each to other swear this moment leaves
Our scales harmonious, neither wanting found
Though weighed in such strict balances. So let
It be with us always. I am too proud
To owe you one caress; you must not drop
Beholden to my favor for one least
Endearing term. Should you reveal some stretch
Of sky to me, let me revive some note
Of music lost to you. This is love's way,
That where a heart is asked gives back a heart.

Portrait of a Lover

Weary, restless, now fever's minion, furnace-hot,
Now without reason shivering prey to some great dread;
Trusting, doubting, prone to reveal, yet wishing not
To name this malady whereby his wits are led,
Trapped in this labyrinth without a magic thread,
He gropes bewildered in a most familiar place;
It should be spring by all the signs and portents spread,
But four strong seasons wrangle on this lover's face.

Of all men born he deems himself so much accurst,
His plight so piteous, his proper pain so rare,
The very bread he eats so dry, so fierce his thirst,
What shall we liken such a martyr to? Compare
Him to a man with poison raging in his throat,
And far away the one mind with an antidote.

An Old Story

"I must be ready when he comes," she said,
"Besieger of the heart, the long adored;
And I shall know him by his regal tread,
And by the grace peculiar to my lord.
Upon my mouth his lips shall be a sword;
Splendid is he by whom this breast shall fall,
This hive of honey burst, this fruit be cored."—
So beauty that would be a willing thrall
Kept vigil, eyes aglow, ear tuned to hear his call.

Had she not had her dream, she might have seen
For what he was the stranger at her gate,
And known his rugged hands, strong mouth, and lean
Hawk-face spelled out for her a star-spun fate.
But captive to a dream she let him wait
In vain for any word she might have said
Whereat he might declare himself her mate.
She looked him through as one unknown or dead;
He passed, an unseen halo blazing round his head.

The grave will be her only lover now,
Though still she watches for the shining one,
Her prince in purple robes, with flaming brow,
Astride a wild steed lineaged from the sun.
Season to season shades, the long days run
To longer years; she still is waiting there,
Not knowing long ago her siege was done,
Not dreaming it has been her bitter share
To entertain her heart's high guest all unaware.

To Lovers of Earth: Fair Warning

Give over to high things the fervent thought
You waste on Earth; let down the righteous bar
Against a wayward peace too dearly bought
Upon this pale and passion-frozen star.
Sweethearts and friends, are they not loyal? Far
More fickle, false, perverse, far more unkind
Is Earth to those who give her heart and mind.

And you whose lusty youth her snares intrigue,
Who glory in her seas, swear by her clouds,
With Age, man's foe, Earth ever is in league.
Time resurrects her even while he crowds
Your bloom to dust, and lengthens out your shrouds
A day's length or a year's; she will be young,
When your last cracked and quivering note is sung.

She will remain the Earth, sufficient still,
Though you are gone and with you that rare loss
That vanishes with your bewildered will.
And there shall flame no red, indignant cross
For you, no quick white scar of wrath emboss
The sky, no blood drip from a wounded moon,
And not a single star chime out of tune.

Varia

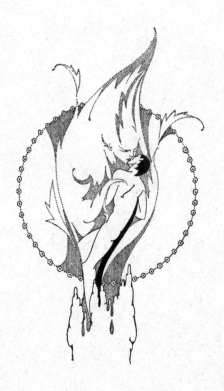

In Spite of Death

All things confirm me in the thought that dust,
Once raised to monumental pride of breath,
To no extent affirms the right of death
To raze such splendor to an ancient crust.
"Grass withereth, the flower fadeth"; yea,
But in the violated seed exults,
The bleakest winter through, a deathless pulse,
Beating, "Spring wipes this sacrilege away."

No less shall I in some new fashion flare
Again, when death has blown my candles out;
Although my blood went down in shameful rout
Tonight, by all this living frame holds fair,
Though death should closet me tonight, I swear
Tomorrow's sun would find his cupboard bare.

Cor Cordium*

Cor cordium is written there,
But the heart of hearts is away;
They could not fashion any bier
To hold that burning clay.

Imprisoned in the flesh, he wrought
Till Death as Prospero,
Pitied the spark that life had caught,
Loosed him, and let him go.

Look, a light like a sun-girt flask;
Listen, and hear it sing.
Light and song are what, you ask?
Ariel off on the wing!

---

* Written at the Shelley Memorial in Rome, August 1926.

Lines to My Father

The many sow, but only the chosen reap;
Happy the wretched host if Day be brief,
That with the cool oblivion of sleep
A dawnless Night may soothe the smart of grief.

If from the soil our sweat enriches sprout
One meagre blossom for our hands to cull,
Accustomed indigence provokes a shout
Of praise that life becomes so bountiful.

Now ushered regally into your own,
Look where you will, as far as eye can see,
Your little seeds are to a fullness grown,
And golden fruit is ripe on every tree.

Yours is no fairy gift, no heritage
Without travail, to which weak wills aspire;
This is a merited and grief-earned wage
From One Who holds His servants worth their hire.

So has the shyest of your dreams come true,
Built not of sand, but of the solid rock,
Impregnable to all that may accrue
Of elemental rage: storm, stress, and shock.

Protest

(To John Trounstine)

I long not now, a little while at least,
For that serene interminable hour
When I shall leave this Barmecidal feast
With poppy for my everlasting flower;
I long not now for that dim cubicle
Of earth to which my lease will not expire,
Where he who comes a tenant there may dwell
Without a thought of famine, flood, or fire.

Surely that house has quiet to bestow—
Still tongue, spent pulse, heart pumped of its last throb,
The fingers tense and tranquil in a row,
The throat unwelled with any sigh or sob—
But time to live, to love, bear pain and smile,
Oh, we are given such a little while!

An Epitaph

(For Amy Lowell)

She leans across a golden table,
   Confronts God with an eye
Still puzzled by the standard label
   All flesh bears: Made to die—
And questions Him if He is able
   To reassure her why.

Scandal and Gossip

Scandal is a stately lady,
Whispers when she talks;
Waves of innuendo
Ripple where she walks.

Speaking with a lifted shoulder,
Flicker of a lash,
Scorning words as dangerous,
She is never rash.

Gossip is a giddy girl
Running here and there,
Showing all the neighborhood
What she has to wear.

Gossip babbles like a brook,
Rages like a flood,
Chews her placid hearsays
As a cow her cud.

Scandal hobnobs with the rich
Over purple wine;
Gossip has the vagabonds
In to chat and dine.

Scandal never visits us;
We are far too poor;
Gossip never missed a day
Knocking at our door.

Youth Sings a Song of Rosebuds

(To Roberta)

Since men grow diffident at last,
And care no whit at all,
If spring be come, or the fall be past,
Or how the cool rains fall,

I come to no flower but I pluck,
I raise no cup but I sip,
For a mouth is the best of sweets to suck;
The oldest wine's on the lip.

If I grow old in a year or two,
And come to the querulous song
Of "Alack and aday" and "This was true,
And that, when I was young,"

I must have sweets to remember by,
Some blossom saved from the mire,
Some death-rebellious ember I
Can fan into a fire.

Hunger

(*To Emerson Withorne*)

Break me no bread however white it be;
It cannot fill the emptiness I know;
No wine can cool this desert thirst in me
Though it had lain a thousand years in snow;
No swooning lotus flower's languid juice
Drips anodyne unto my restlessness,
And impotent to win me to a truce
Is every artifice of loveliness.
Inevitable is the way I go,
False-faced amid a pageant permeate
With bliss, yet visioning a higher wave
Than this weak ripple washing to and fro;
The fool still keeps his dreams inviolate
Till their virginity espouse the grave.

Lines to Our Elders

(*To Melanie*)

You too listless to examine
If in pestilence or famine
Death lurk least, a hungry gamin
Gnawing on you like a beaver
On a root, while you trifle
Time away nodding in the sun,
Careless how the shadows crawl
Surely up your crumbling wall,
Heedless of the Thief's footfall,
Death's whose nimble fingers rifle
Your heartbeats one by weary one,—
Here's the difference in our dying:
You go dawdling, we go flying.
Here's a thought flung out to plague you:
Ours the pleasure if we'd liever
Burn completely with the fever
Than go ambling with the ague.

The Poet

Lest any forward thought intrude
Of death and desolation,
Upon a mind shaped but to brood
On wonder and creation,
He keeps an unremittent feud
Against such usurpation.

His ears are tuned to all sharp cries
Of travail and complaining,
His vision stalks a new moon's rise
In every old moon's waning,
And in his heart pride's red flag flies
Too high for sorrow's gaining.

Thus militant, with sword in hand,
His battle shout renewing,
He feels all faith affords is planned,
As seeds, for rich accruing;
Death ties no knot too gordianed
For his deft hands' undoing.

More Than a Fool's Song

(*To Edward Perry*)

Go look for beauty where you least
Expect to hear her hive;
Regale your belly with a feast
Of hunger till you thrive.

For honest treatment seek the thief;
For truth consult the liar;
Court pleasure in the halls of grief;
Find smoothness on a briar.

The worth impearled in chastity
Is known best of the harlot,
And courage throws her panoply
On many a native varlet.

In Christian practice those who move
To symbols strange to us
May reckon clearer of His love
Than we who own His cross.

The world's a curious riddle thrown
Water-wise from heaven's cup;
The souls we think are hurtling down
Perhaps are climbing up.

And When I Think

(*For one just dead*)

And when I think how that dark throat of thine,
Irreconcilably stilled, lies mute,
A golden honey-hive robbed of its fruit,
A wassail cup in which there is no wine;
Thy sweet, high treble hushed that never mine
Auricular delight again shall suit
To wild bird warblings, or liken to a flute
That with wild tremors agitates the spine;
Then though the legion-throated spring cry out,
Though raucously the summer whirl about
Me all her scent and color in one shout
Of pride, though autumn clamor at my ear,
Or winter crackle round me, crystal-clear,
While memory persists, I do not hear.

Advice to a Beauty

(*To Sydonia*)

Of all things, lady, be not proud;
Inter not beauty in that shroud
Wherein the living waste, the dead,
Unwept and unrememberéd,
Decay. Beauty beats so frail a wing;
Suffer men to gaze, poets to sing
How radiant you are, compare
And favor you to that most rare
Bird of delight: a lovely face
Matched with an equal inner grace.
Sweet bird, beware the Fowler, Pride;
His knots once neatly crossed and tied,
The prey is caged and walled about
With no way in and no way out.

Ultimatum

I hold not with the fatalist creed
Of what must be must be;
There is enough to meet my need
In this most meagre me.

These two slim arms were made to rein
My steed, to ward and fend;
There is more gold in this small brain
Than I can ever spend.

The seed I plant is chosen well;
Ambushed by no sly sweven,
I plant it if it droops to hell,
Or if it blooms to heaven.

Lines Written in Jerusalem*

A city builded on a hill may flaunt
Its glory in the sunken valley's face,
And ways the Nazarene has trod may vaunt
A credible inheritance of grace.
Your very stones, Jerusalem, can sing:
"He would have taken us beneath His wing."

---

* August 1926

On the Mediterranean Sea*

That weaver of words, the poet who
First named this sullen sea the blue,
And left off painting there, he knew
How rash a man would be to try
Precise defining of such a dye
As lurks within this colored spume.
And for retelling little room
He willed to singers then unborn
But destined later years, at morn,
High noon, twilight, or night to view
This Protean sheet, and anguish through
The mind to paint its wayward hue.
Not Helen's eyes, no vaunted stains
That shone in Cressid's lacy veins,
Not those proud fans the peacocks spread,
No sky that ever arched its head
Above a wonder-stricken two
Aghast at love, wore such a hue.
Only the Hand that never erred
Bent on beauty, creation-spurred,
Could mix and mingle such a dye,
Nor leave its like in earth or sky.
That sire of singers, the poet who
First named this sullen sea the blue
And left off painting there, he knew!

* July 15, 1926

Millennial

(*To John Haynes Holmes*)

Once in a thousand years a call may ring
Divested so of every cumbering lie,
A man espousing it may fight and sing,
And count it but a little thing to die;
Once in a thousand years a star may come,
Six-pointed, tipped with such an astral flow,
Its singing sisters must bow hushed in dumb,
Half-mutinous, yet half-adoring show.

Once in as many years a man may rise
So cosmopolitan of thought and speech,
Humanity reflected in his eyes,
His heart a haven every race can reach,
That doubters shall receive a mortal thrust,
And own, "This man proves flesh exalts its dust."

At the Wailing Wall in Jerusalem

Of all the grandeur that was Solomon's
High testament of Israel's far pride,
Shedding its lustre like a sun of suns,
This feeble flicker only has not died.
This wall alone reminds a vanquished race,
This brief remembrance still retained in stone,
That sure foundations guard their given place
To rehabilitate the overthrown.

So in the battered temple of the heart,
That grief is harder on than time on stone,
Though three sides crumble, one will stand apart,
Where thought may mourn its past, remembrance groan,
And hands now bare that once were rich with rings
Rebuild upon the ancient site of things.

To Endymion*

Endymion, your star is steadfast now,
Beyond aspersion's power to glitter down;
There is no redder blossom on the bough
Of song, no richer jewel in her crown;
Long shall she stammer forth a broken note,
(Striving with how improvident a tongue)
Before the ardor of another throat
Transcends the jubilate you have sung.

High as the star of that last poignant cry
Death could not stifle in the wasted frame,
You know at length the bright immortal lie
Time gives to those detractors of your name,
And see, from where you and Diana ride,
Your humble epitaph—how misapplied!

---

* Rome, August 1926, after a visit to the grave of Keats.

Epilogue

The lily, being white not red,
  Contemns the vivid flower,
And men alive believe the dead
  Have lost their vital power.

Yet some prefer the brilliant shade,
  And pass the livid by;
And no man knows if dead men fade
  Or bloom, save those that die.

Juvenilia

Open Door

Once I held my heart's door full wide
That love might enter in;
I saw him pass in peacock pride,
Nor cast a glance within.

The door stands wide by night and day,
The lamp burns on though dim,
Lest some lone traveler lose his way.
(Love thinks it burns for him.)

Disenchantment

This is the circle fairies drew
To hold your love and mine,
And here it was the tall tree grew
With fruit we bruised for wine.

Serene we stand where once we stood
Scarce breathing, tense, alert;
Now nothing stirs for ill or good,
For healing or for hurt.

Your hands are cold, and I am cold;
We speak, but drop no pearls;
No careless wind disturbs the gold
Still cradled in your curls.

Call—yet no agile echo leaps
A mountain for our grief;
No slant-eyed fawn for terror creeps
    long a trembling leaf.

If once I had a fairy club,
You had a wonder stone,
And did I wave or you but rub,
The world was all our own.

This is the circle; see, I wave
My wand, you rub your stone;
But nothing's here except a grave
On which cold winds have blown.

Leaves

One, two, and three,
Dead leaves drift from a tree.

Yesterday they loved
Wind and rain, the brush
Of wings
Soft and clean, that moved
Through them beyond the crush
Of things.
Yesterday they loved.

Yesterday they sang
Silver symphonies,
Raised high
Holy chants that rang
Leaf-wise through their trees;
As I,
Yesterday they sang.

Unremembered now,
They will soon lie warm
With snow;
They could grace a bough
Once, and love and charm,
Although
Unremembered now.

Trees so soon forget
Little leaves they had
Before,
Knowing spring will let
Them wake, vernal clad
With more;
Trees so soon forget.

Man dreams that he
Is more than a leaf on a tree.

Song

Love, unto me be song of bird;
So soon the song is through;
I would I had a brazen word
To brand this truth untrue.

Love, unto me be life's full sun,
Unmindful of your light;
So soon the stealthy shadows run
All days into one night.

There is a word that must be spoken,
A word your heart would hear,
And mine must whisper, or be broken;
Oh, make your heart your ear.

The Touch

I am no longer lame since Spring
Stooped to me where I lay,
And charmed with flute and silver lute
My laggard limbs to play.
Her voice is sweet as long-stored wine;
I leap like a hounded fawn;
I rise and follow over hill and hollow
To the flush of the crimson dawn!

A Poem Once Significant,
Now Happily Not

Whatever I have loved has wounded me;
I bear unto my grave this crimson scar,
The vivid testament of how a star
Can hurt; and I am blinded by the sea.
Hell-deep and heaven-high for Beauty's sake,
Pierced with the shaft that rankles ere it kills,
I danced with dawn and dusk upon their hills,
Yet thought at each earth kiss my heart would break.

Small wonder is it, love, that you who are
Far lovelier than sea, dawn-flush, or star,
Or spittled clay grown arrogant with breath,
Beholding this maimed thing that dares to crawl
To your imperial bosom, should let fall
Your hand, betrothing Insolence to Death.

Under the Mistletoe

I did not know she'd take it so,
Or else I'd never dared;
Although the bliss was worth the blow,
I did not know she'd take it so.
She stood beneath the mistletoe
So long I thought she cared;
I did not know she'd take it so,
Or else I'd never dared.